Original title:
The Ocean's Enchantment

Copyright © 2025 Creative Arts Management OÜ
All rights reserved.

Author: Gideon Barrett
ISBN HARDBACK: 978-1-80587-423-2
ISBN PAPERBACK: 978-1-80587-893-3

Celestial Waters

The fish throw parties in their finny attire,
With bubbles of laughter, they never tire.
Underwater conga lines twist and swerve,
As octopuses dance, they really have verve.

Seahorses gossip, spinning tales so grand,
Whales are the DJs, making waves on demand.
Starfish applaud with their five-pointed limbs,
While jellyfish glow like delightfully dimmed hymns.

The Tempest's Lullaby

A crab plays the drums on a shipwrecked sail,
While clams sing sweet songs to the wind's wild wail.
The seagulls squawk jokes, making sailors grin,
As thunder claps along, it's their favorite din.

The skies heave sighs, unable to stay mad,
For dolphins leap high, oh, isn't it rad?
Rain turns to laughter, splashing all around,
In this whimsical whirl, joy knows no bound.

Glistening Horizons

The sun sets in colors that tickle the eye,
As crabs throw maracas and seagulls all fly.
Each wave shares a story, a laugh and a tease,
While shells serve up snacks amid the gentle breeze.

Surfboards go sliding with a giggle and splash,
As snails in sun hats take a leisurely dash.
The sand takes a nap while the sun winks bright,
In this shimmering scene, everything feels right.

Mermaid's Melody

A mermaid hums tunes that tickle the sea,
With dolphins chiming in, oh so merrily.
Starfish tap dance on the coral so fine,
As clowns of the reef take a hilarious line.

Her party's a splash, with crabs serving pie,
While fish attempt limbo, oh my, oh my!
The moonlight chuckles, reflecting their glee,
In this underwater world, joyous and free.

Hushed Waters

In quiet depths where flippers leap,
A fish forgot his usual sleep.
He danced a jig, all out of time,
Claiming he could swim and rhyme.

The crabs applauded with their claws,
While seaweed swayed without a pause.
"Let's start a band!" the shrimp did shout,
But a seahorse just swam about.

Sun-Kissed Shores

On sandy banks with shells galore,
A hermit crab just begged for more.
He tried a hat that fit just right,
But it rolled away, oh what a sight!

Sunburned jelly, a comical spree,
Shared its tales of wobbly glee.
"Let's have a party, bring your best joke!"
But every punchline turned to smoke.

Shadows Beneath the Waves

Beneath the waves where shadows play,
A turtle snored the night away.
The octopus with colors bright,
Painted its dreams in sheer delight.

An eel with puns would twist and turn,
While fishy friends would laugh and yearn.
"Who's that snoring? Is it a whale?"
"Nope, it's just Ted, with his funny tale!"

Lighthouses and Longing

A lighthouse blinked with jokes galore,
Sending beams across the shore.
"Hey boat, don't you take a wrong turn!
I'll dim my light for a laugh to burn!"

A sailor chuckled, "What a shine!"
As waves spouted with salty wine.
With each wave crash, they laughed anew,
While a seagull squawked, "Hey, I like blue!"

Whispers of the Wind

The seagulls gossip without a care,
They squawk about treasures and fish so rare.
A starfish once tried to dance in a twirl,
But slipped on the sand and gave quite a whirl.

The crabs hold a meeting, all dressed in shells,
Arguing if seaweed is good, oh do tell!
A dolphin sneaks by, playing tricks on the whales,
While a clam just sits tight, with it's secrets and tales.

Currents of Time

Now jellyfish float like balloons in the air,
While sea turtles giggle at fish without care.
A clam and an octopus had quite a feud,
Over who looked better in a shell 'dude.'

The tide rolls in with a whoosh and a splash,
While seahorses race, oh they're lightning fast!
But octopuses laugh, saying 'time is a game,'
As they juggle their limbs—it's all kind of lame.

The Rhythm of the Sea

The seashells hum tunes in a playful beat,
As hermit crabs march with taps on their feet.
A fish tried to sing, but forgot all the notes,
While the coral recruits with their colorful coats.

A surfboard decided to join in the fun,
Riding the waves just to see how they run.
The tides rolled their eyes, saying 'not today,
We've got our own rhythm, so go on, shoosh away!'

Beliefs in the Blue

The barnacles whisper tales old and true,
Of ships that once sailed on oceans of blue.
A mermaid's dilemma of hair and of sea,
Should she braid it or let it float wild and free?

A grouper believed he was king of the tide,
Until a big whale told him, 'better glide!
For the ocean holds secrets, they ebb and they flow,
And humor reminds us that life's such a show!"

Ocean's Heartbeat

The waves dance wildly, a fish in a hat,
A crab in a tux, what do you think of that?
Seagulls wear sunglasses, looking quite cool,
While starfish play poker, breaking every rule.

So grab a shell phone, let's call the sea,
Fishy friends laughing, they welcome you and me.
With bubbles for giggles and kelp for a snack,
We'll sail on a shoal, no need to look back.

Nautical Serenade

A whale with a ukulele strums with delight,
As jellyfish jiggle in the moonlight.
Clams serenade us with a soft, sweet tune,
While dolphins dive deeper, under the moon.

The octopus juggles with style and grace,
While turtles chuckle, slack-jawed at space.
A snail sings a ballad, slow and sincere,
While mermaids sip seaweed, laughing with cheer.

Abyssal Wonders

Deep down where the strange and wiggly roam,
An anglerfish frowns, he's far from home.
He invites a squid, known for his flair,
To join in the antics of a sea monster fair.

The flatfish tell tales, all flat and absurd,
Of a crab who once danced without saying a word.
With bubbles as popcorn, and barnacles cheer,
Even the sea cucumbers laugh without fear.

The Horizon's Embrace

As sunsets ignite like a painter's bold stroke,
The pirates share stories, each one a joke.
Their parrots squawk loudly, a raucous refrain,
While mermaids roll on, just trying to regain.

The sun dips down low, like a lazy cat,
And fish tell tall tales of adventures they've had.
With laughter a-plenty and smiles all around,
The horizon's their playground; what joy can be found!

Soliloquy at Dusk

The sun dips low, a golden tease,
Seagulls dance with whims like breeze.
Shells complain in a crabby tone,
'Who stole my shine? I'm all alone!'

Waves whisper secrets, cheeky and sly,
'Is that a fish or just my tie?'
Mermaids giggle, they've lost their flair,
Playing tag with a hapless bear.

Floating past on a beach ball dream,
A starfish dreams of a seated scheme.
Mollusks sigh and roll their eyes,
'Life's a wave of goofy ties!'

Stories from the Shoreline

Crabs wear crowns and strut around,
While starfish scoff, 'We're ocean-bound!'
A wise old turtle tells a joke,
'Why don't fish ever play poke?'

The sand's a stage, shells make a band,
Playing tunes that tickle the sand.
A dolphin dives with a splashy grin,
'Try to catch me, good luck with that swim!'

Children laugh as waves chase their feet,
'Run, run, the wave's got bad feet!'
Seagulls caw a comic show,
'We've got more flair than you could know!'

Beyond the Horizon

Far away the sailboats dance,
While jellyfish think it's a romance.
Octopus juggles with broad, eight hands,
'Get your popcorn! This is grand!'

Seashells gossip in hushed delight,
'Have you seen the fish with a bright light?'
Tides roll in with a laugh and smirk,
'Watch out, beachgoers, here comes the quirk!'

A floating log waves like a friend,
'The beach is strange, it does not end!'
Gulls squawk, 'We're the kings of the sea,'
'But don't tell the fish, they might disagree!'

Odes to the Tide

Oh wavy dance of the playful sea,
Crabs are fashionistas, can't you see?
Lobsters sport their snazziest claws,
'Check out my grip, where are your jaws?'

Waves roll in with a boisterous cheer,
'Can you hear us? We're quite sincere!'
'Your sunscreen's gone, it's quite a plight,'
'Well, that's just perfect, it feels just right!'

Tidal pools hold the best of shows,
Knock knock! Who's there? Anemone knows!
Seaweed giggles, swaying with glee,
'Life's a beach party, come dance with me!'

Phosphorescent Nights

Underneath the glowing waves,
Squid dance like they're in cafes.
Crabs wear hats and strut their stuff,
While jellyfish giggle, saying, 'Tough!'

Mermen dive to catch a wave,
In bubble shoes that look quite brave.
But seahorses steal the show,
With tiny surfboards, on they go!

Starfish play the ukulele,
While octopi snap selfies, gaily.
Clams throw parties—no clamshells!
Undersea, where laughter swells!

So if you seek a midnight spree,
Come and join our jamboree.
The ocean's quirks bring joy anew,
With phosphorescent laughs, just for you!

Driftwood Dreams

A driftwood log in sunshine beams,
Becomes a ship for childish dreams.
Fish hold parties with some flair,
While turtles zoom past without a care!

Seashells whisper silly tales,
Of pirate ships and wind-filled sails.
A crab insists he's captain bold,
But flips his hat when he gets cold!

Dolphins surf on wine corks sweet,
As mermaids play on seaweed feet.
The breeze carries laughter, clear and bright,
In this driftwood world, all feels right.

So grab your dreams and float along,
In driftwood realms, where you belong.
With every wave, a chuckle grows,
As the ocean's humor overflows!

Cartography of the Currents

With maps drawn on the ocean's floor,
Squid sketch routes from shore to shore.
They giggle at their own fine art,
As starfish critique with a wise heart.

The currents swirl like raucous pens,
Drawing paths for fishy friends.
A pufferfish shows off his ink,
But his map makes everyone rethink!

Turtles follow guidelines, slow,
While clueless lobsters steal the show.
They venture off the beaten line,
Chasing bubbles, feeling fine!

In this land of nautical wit,
Where charts are drawn with a splashy fit,
Join the fun as the sea unfolds,
In currents mapped with laughter bold!

Siren's Call

A siren sang in giggles bright,
Her pitch a joke, her tunes a fright.
She lured the sailors, made them gleam,
But turned their ships to seafoam cream!

With every note, she tossed a tease,
Making fish laugh, as light as breeze.
The sailors danced, they didn't know,
They were the stars of her big show!

Her voice like bubbles—pops and fizz,
On boats where no one quite knows whiz.
Fortune cookies made afloat,
As sea creatures wrote her a funny note.

So if you hear a chuckling song,
Know it's a siren singing wrong!
But join the fun, don't be too sad,
For laughter's the treasure to be had!

The Siren's Whisper

In a shell, I found a sound,
A fishy tune, it spun around.
It sang of crabs in fancy shoes,
And offered me a pair to choose.

A mermaid winked with scales that shimmer,
Her seashell bra made seagulls glimmer.
"Join our dance, oh land-bound fellow!"
I tripped and fell - oh what a bellow!

With jellyfish doing the cha-cha slide,
I swung my arms, but bumped a tide.
The starfish laughed, it seemed to say,
"Don't quit your day job, dance another way!"

The seashell band began to play,
While seaweed swayed in bright array.
With dolphins diving, oh what cheer!
But watch your step, or grab a beer!

Shades of the Deep

The snails in shades, they take a stroll,
Their shells so bright, they stole the role.
A crab with swag, it clicks and clacks,
Said, "Join my crew, we need some snacks!"

Behind a rock, the octopus hid,
In silly socks, what a weird bid!
He waved hello with eight long arms,
And whispered "Let's devise some charms!"

With sea cucumbers as my crew,
We plotted ways to swim anew.
A tuna winked, a prankster glum,
And loosed the bubbles—what a scrum!

The jelly beans made jelly grins,
While seagulls squawked their silly sins.
We laughed so hard, I lost my breath,
In hues of blue, we danced to death!

Starlit Sea Drifts

Under the waves, the stars do glow,
A fish, a judge, gave me a show.
He ruled on clams and silly tides,
While crabs in wigs gave fun-filled rides.

The angler with his light so bright,
Tried to show off all through the night.
He caught a little fish so sly,
It slipped away with a cheeky lie.

With plankton disco balls around,
The sea turtles grooved without a sound.
A dolphin's flip, oh what a sight,
We swam in circles, pure delight!

Luminous waves rolled with a jest,
"Catch me if you can!" they said with zest.
But slippery fun in water's gleam,
Let's leave some chaos for a dream!

The Tranquil Abyss

Down below where sunlight weeps,
The clam had secrets, oh so deep.
He whispered tales of treasure's might,
But hid them well, oh what a sight!

A puffer fish with quite the flair,
Puffed up big beyond compare.
He popped a balloon and gave a shout,
"Let's paint the sea, let's twist about!"

I met a turtle with a quirk,
He offered snacks with quite a smirk.
"Try my seaweed, it's a hit!"
One bite and I fell into a fit!

So watch your step in waters calm,
For laughter swims and sings a balm.
In tranquil depths, where fun is rife,
A goofy fish brought me to life!

Secrets of the Seafloor

Bubbles rise with tales untold,
Where crabs do dance in shells so bold.
A fish in glasses swims by day,
Saying, "I lost my way to play!"

A starfish tries to do a jig,
But ends up just a lazy gig.
As mermaids giggle, spinning round,
A treasure chest lets out a sound!

Seahorses ride a current's tune,
With seaweed hats, they'll dance till noon.
An octopus with eight left feet,
Says, "I've got moves for you to meet!"

The seafloor is a crazy scene,
With playful pranks that make you scream.
So dive right in and join the fun,
The depths of laughter have begun!

A Symphony of Salty Breezes

The gulls are shrieking in delight,
As crabs form bands in full moonlight.
The seaweed sways to rhythms grand,
With conch shells blown by sandy hands.

A clam has lost its favorite beat,
While dolphins twirl on whiskered feet.
The fishes join with giddy squeaks,
In harmony that laughs and peaks.

The waves act as a quirky drum,
As water lizards tap and strum.
A whale brings bass, oh what a blast,
It's, "Who needs silence?!" from the past!

In salty breezes, laughs abound,
With every dance, new joys are found.
Come join this orchestra of cheer,
Where even silence brings a jeer!

The Coral Kingdom

In coral castles, fish parade,
With every wave, a grand charade.
The jellyfish wear gowns of glow,
While seahorses steal the show!

Crabs wearing crowns strut down the way,
Declaring, "Today's the best of days!"
A clownfish giggles, cracks a joke,
While turtles laugh and puff out smoke.

The sea cucumbers conga line,
Swaying to the rhythm just divine.
A shipwreck's treasure forms a band,
With every note, they take a stand!

In the kingdom where the colors burst,
Every funny fish quenches its thirst.
So come and frolic, dance around,
In coral depths, joy knows no bounds!

Reflections on the Surface

The mirror of the water gleams,
Where silly fish enact their dreams.
A dolphin flips, a twirling spree,
And laughs at its own reflection, see!

A crab with shades sits on the shore,
Sipping on cocktails, wanting more.
Flipping through shells, they find some gold,
But toss it back, it's just too bold!

A seagull swoops, starts a rock band,
With catchy tunes made from the sand.
From every splash, a chuckle flows,
Where laughter sparkles, joy just grows.

So on the surface, life's a tease,
With every ripple offering ease.
Embrace the fun, let laughter soar,
In the watery world, life's never a bore!

Legends of the Deep Blue

There once was a fish with a hat,
Who fancied himself quite a brat.
He swam past a whale,
Made a joke on a scale,
And challenged the crabs to a spat.

A turtle named Terry was slow,
He boasted about his great show.
But when he took flight,
He landed in fright,
Claiming seaweed was just for the blow.

A seahorse danced wearing a shoe,
He twirled in a whirl, what a view!
They laughed with glee,
At the sight of the sea,
With tales of the tide, always new.

So join in the fun of the waves,
Where laughter breaks free from the caves.
Each creature a star,
In their own quirky bazaar,
In deep blue, they dazzle and rave.

Aquamarine Tryst

A crab wore a tie, thinking grand,
While planning a trip to the sand.
He danced with a clam,
Said, 'You're my jam!',
As they frolicked and skipped hand in hand.

A mermaid with hair made of foam,
Sang tunes that would tickle your dome.
She tripped on a wave,
Shouting, 'I'm brave!',
And splashed all the fish in her home.

The octopus planned a big feast,
Inviting the jellyfish for a treat.
But all of his dishes,
Were made out of wishes,
And tasted like bubblegum yeast.

So gather the friends from the sea,
For laughter, and one big jubilee.
With jesters galore,
And fish on the floor,
A party like none you would see.

Gems of the Shore

A starfish with five tiny feet,
Dreamed of dancing to a big beat.
He tried to break out,
But threw in a pout,
Claiming sand made it hard to compete.

A walrus with a big goofy grin,
Thought surfing was surely a win.
He jumped on a wave,
Said, 'Look, I'm brave!',
And fell with a splash and a spin.

The seagulls were squawking a tune,
As the sun set beneath the blue moon.
With feathers in flight,
They laughed at the sight,
Of a crab guest performing at noon.

So treasure the laughs from the tide,
Where silliness flows far and wide.
With friends all around,
In joy, we are bound,
In the gems of the shore, we reside.

Seafarer's Reverie

A sailor dreamed of goldfish stew,
And claimed it was fine for a crew.
But when they all tried,
They laughed and then cried,
Saying, 'Captain, we've all gone askew!'

A parrot who talked like a bard,
Said jokes that left sailors charred.
He squawked with delight,
As a dolphin took flight,
And both played a game of discard.

A jellyfish wore a top hat,
Complaining, 'This style's where it's at!'
But each time he'd sway,
He'd drift far away,
Chasing seahorses, look at that!

So raise up your glass to the sea,
Where goofiness flows wild and free.
In dreams of the wave,
We all misbehave,
For laughter is best in the spree.

The Silent Deep

Bubbles rise with a silly squeak,
As fish in tuxedos play hide and peek.
A crab can't dance, he moves with a clatter,
While seaweed giggles, 'Hey, what's the matter?'

The octopus juggles shells on his head,
While seahorses prance, they've got no dread.
But watch out, a dolphin plays a prank,
With a splash and a wiggle, he draws a blank.

A mermaid laughs with a glistening tail,
Telling fishy jokes that never seem pale.
The waters sing with a gurgle and cheer,
In this hidden realm, there's nothing to fear.

So come take a dip, let your worries subside,
With friends who are finned and giggles worldwide.
Join in the fun, in the shimmer and foam,
In this crazy deep, you'll feel right at home.

Orcas and Opal Shores

Orcas in bow ties float by with style,
Chasing their tails, they swim quite a mile.
They joke about jellyfish doing a jig,
While clams wiggle up like they're dancing big.

At opal shores where the waves just giggle,
A starfish sings tunes while a kid tries to wiggle.
A crab holds a seaweed mic in his claw,
And everyone tunes into nature's law.

A sandcastle stands with a flag on the top,
Still, seagulls swoop in – wait! Did they just stop?
They squawk out a tune with no sense of tone,
But beachgoers grin; it's a concert of stone!

With laughter and splashes, the day rolls away,
As orcas and kids join in for the play.
Oh, what a riot, this seaside delight,
In the sparkly strands of the sun's golden light.

Moons over Marinas

Under a moon so bright and round,
Fish throw a party with no sense of sound.
Starfish DJ spins a tune with a flip,
While seagulls do the electric shuffle and trip.

With a splash and a grin, the boats all sway,
As crabs in tuxedos join in the fray.
"Yo ho ho!" cries a shrimp with a flair,
While dolphins all chuckle, floating on air.

Sailboats are bobbing in playful delight,
With glow-in-the-dark anchors shining so bright.
A clam sings the blues, well, sort of off-key,
But everyone's dancing so wild and so free!

As the moon dips low, the night wears a crown,
With laughter and joy, nobody frowns.
Curfew? No way! Let the fun never cease,
In the moonlit marina, all worries release.

Shores of Solitude

On shores where the laughter echoes afar,
A dogfish plays fetch with a whimsical star.
Seashells are scattered, each tells a tale,
Of merfolk who giggle and fish off the rail.

A turtle in shades slowly struts with panache,
While crabs strut their stuff, oh, such a fine clash!
The pelicans lounge, sipping seashell cocktails,
As starry-eyed fish share adventure-filled tales.

In the seafoam's tickle, secrets unfold,
Of sea creature antics and treasures of gold.
A playful otter slides down a soft wave,
Laughing away all the worries we save.

So come to these shores, where solitude's fun,
With whimsical critters in the warm setting sun.
Beauty and mirth hand in fin, oh so right,
At the shore's tender edge, pure delight takes flight.

Mysteries of the Abyss

In the deep, where the fish wear hats,
And crabs play poker with silly spats,
A whale sings songs that tickle your toes,
While jellyfish waltz in extravagant clothes.

The octopus juggles, a real sight to see,
He'll show you his tricks, just give him a tea.
The starfish giggles, sits bold on a rock,
Counting the bubbles that dance 'round the clock.

A turtle in shades lounges all day,
Reminds little fish to come out and play.
With pearls of wisdom in watery chime,
They'll share every secret, all in good time.

So dive in with laughter, don't be a bore,
In the deep blue, there's always much more!

Nautical Nightfall

As the moonlight glimmers on waves full of cheer,
Seagulls are laughing, it's party time here.
With dolphins playing a game of charades,
And mermaids sharing their sweet lemonade.

The sea turtles groan as they try to glide,
In wobbly dance moves, oh what a ride!
While crabs in tuxedos take turns in a race,
Claiming the title with a sidestep embrace.

Starfish spin tales of treasure and glee,
Each one more ridiculous, as funny as can be.
A big fish retorts, 'I've seen them before!'
But they just keep chuckling, wanting more lore.

So as night casts shadows and waves gently crash,
Join in the laughter, let none of it pass!

Dance of the Water Spirits

In a whirl of splashes, the sprites take the stage,
With flips and twirls to amuse every age.
A mermaid does cartwheels, her hair in a whirl,
While sea urchins cheer for their favorite girl.

The waves join the rhythm, a binary beat,
As crabs form a train with those tiny little feet.
The seaweed's a partner, swaying with grace,
Every twirl bringing smiles to every sea face.

Then suddenly, a sea monster joins in,
Who would have thought he could dance with such spin?
But laughter erupts through the shimmering night,
As bubbles float freely, oh what a sight!

So dive into the fun with a splash and a cheer,
For when spirits are rising, there's nothing to fear!

Cascading Rhythms

With every tide that rolls in with a grin,
The fish form a choir, they sing from within.
They bubble and gurgle, the songs feel so right,
As sea cucumbers join in with delight.

A clam snaps its shell in a silly refrain,
While snappy little shrimp join in the campaign.
A conch shell lays low, claiming secondhand fame,
Yet the flounders proclaim they've mastered the game.

The waves start to ripple, the sea foam takes flight,
As the sun sets below, casting sparkles of light.
Seashells might giggle, if they hadering ears,
'Cause laughter can be heard for miles, never fears.

So join in the rhythms, let nonsense ensue,
For the cheeky sea spirits are waiting for you!

Secrets of the Coastal Breeze

Seagulls squawk as I eat my fries,
They dive and swoop, oh what a surprise!
A crab waves back, with a pinch of glee,
As I dance with sunscreen and sand on my knee.

Waves tickle toes and flip flops fly,
An octopus laughs, oh me, oh my!
Beach balls bounce, like jellyfish on land,
Life's a beach party, come join the band!

The sun's a jester, with rays that tease,
It promises tan lines, so hard to please!
With every splash and silly fall,
It's a laugh-a-minute, come one, come all!

Shells tell tales beneath the sun,
Of treasures lost and races run.
In coastal whispers, secrets swim,
A fishy chorus, let us join in!

A Thousand Sea Stories

From pirates' gold to mermaid's hair,
The stories sparkle beyond compare.
A dolphin flipped and waved goodbye,
While a clam grabbed pearls with a wink of an eye.

Seashells giggle as they share their lore,
About the fish that flew and others that snore.
The tide's a bard, with tales so grand,
Of crabs in capes who rule the sand.

A curious turtle, slow but wise,
Told secrets hidden beneath blue skies.
With every wave, a tale unfolds,
Of underwater antics, quite bold!

So raise a glass of salty cheer,
To tales of the sea, let's lend an ear!
With snickers and splashes, we dance and sway,
In a world where laughter won't slip away!

The Dance of Dolphins

In the bright blue, dolphins prance,
With flips and spins, they love to dance.
They wear their joy like shiny hats,
While seaweed wiggles, thinking it's that!

Waves applaud with a foamy roar,
As dolphins shout, "Give us more!"
With every splash and comedic dive,
They bubble with laughter, so alive!

Caught on a wave, they steal the show,
Making sure their fun does grow.
They twirl and swirl beneath the sun,
A watery ballet, oh what fun!

So join their dance on summer days,
Where silliness flows in countless ways.
With dolphins leading a merry spree,
Let your heart leap like a fish in glee!

Elysian Waters

On the shore where the sand is soft,
The water whispers, just like a soft loft.
A starfish grins with a goofy face,
In the sun's warm embrace, we find our place.

Jellyfish float, what a funny sight,
In their squishy suits, they glide with delight.
As beachgoers giggle and take a dip,
The ocean teases with a gentle tip!

Oh, jelly sandals squeak and slide,
With every wave, we take that ride.
Crabs share jokes with a sideways glance,
And seaweed sways in a silly dance.

So here's to the waters, both deep and blue,
With laughter and joy, they welcome you.
In this coastal realm, let's play our part,
With waves of giggles that fill the heart!

Dance of the Seafoam

A bubble rises, oh so grand,
It lands on folks like grains of sand.
With a jig and a wiggly wave,
They all dance like they're in a rave.

The seagulls laugh, flapping their wings,
As humans slip, doing silly things.
A splash here, a splash there, what fun!
Who knew dancing was 'under the sun'?

Seaweed sways, it's groovy too,
Joining in like a trusty crew.
With every wiggle, a new surprise,
The ocean giggles under blue skies.

So come and join, don't be shy,
Let the salty breeze tickle your thigh.
Let's waltz with crabs on the shore,
And laugh till we can laugh no more!

Mysteries Beneath the Surface

What's hiding down there in the deep?
A clam with secrets it wants to keep?
Maybe a fish with a funny hat,
Or a crab that struts, oh imagine that!

Dolphins play charades all day,
While eels give side-eyes, come what may.
A turtle's tale, ancient and wise,
Could leave you puzzled with wide-eyed surprise.

Shells may whisper, "What's your game?"
As jellyfish float, never the same.
And a starfish grins, arms all akimbo,
"Everything's better with a splash and a limbo!"

So dive right in, or at least pretend,
You'll find the weird and wacky blend.
Each treasure's a giggle, a bubble, a glee,
To summon the joys of what's under the sea!

Siren's Call at Dusk

A melody drifts, soft and sweet,
With fish doing the cha-cha on slippery feet.
"Come dance with me!" the sirens croon,
While shells clap along beneath the moon.

But wait, what's that? A fish in a dress?
Sashing by with an air of finesse.
He twirls and he swirls, all a-glow,
"Who knew the sea could put on such a show?"

Seagulls mock with a cackle and squawk,
As they join the dance on a nearby rock.
And somewhere a mermaid is sipping her tea,
While the waves ripple gossip with glee.

So heed ye the call, come join the fun,
In this watery world where laughter's begun.
With a wink, a splash, it's a party divine,
Let the music of waves make your worries decline!

Where Currents Dream

In depths where the currents wave and sway,
Fishes play hide and seek all day.
A dolphin giggles and spins with glee,
"Catch me if you can, just wait and see!"

Barnacles chime, like bells on parade,
Creating a concert, an oceanic charade.
And octopuses juggle their breakfast delight,
While underwater creatures dance through the night.

A crab wears a crown, his smile so wide,
With a royal wave, he commands the tide.
But what of the sharks? They're just in a trance,
Joining the fun with a goofy dance!

So float on the waves and dream with all might,
The sea's funny tales will bring you delight.
In the currents, you'll find joy wrapped in foam,
Where every ripple can feel just like home!

Waves Whisper Secrets

Waves roll in with playful glee,
Telling tales of fish and sea.
Listen close, they burble bold,
Secrets of the deep unfold.

Crabs in sandals dance and prance,
Seagulls join in a wacky trance.
They gossip in saltwater slang,
While dolphins giggle and sing with a bang.

Buckets and shovels, what a sight,
Sandcastles built with sheer delight.
But watch out for the sneaky tide,
It jokes and splashes, in fun it'll slide.

In this world, jesters and jest,
Nature's humor is truly the best.
So grab your floatie, ride the wave,
At gulls' laughter, be brave, be brave!

Celestial Tides

Stars twinkle in the evening sky,
As waves create an ocean sigh.
The moon in laughter starts to roll,
Pulling tides, it plays the fool.

Crabs wear hats, it's quite the scene,
While mermaids giggle, sharp and keen.
They do the limbo on seaweed strands,
With starfish clapping their tiny hands.

At dusk, the tide calls out to fish,
'Join our party, it's your wish!'
They shimmy and shake, all scales and fins,
In the dance of life, the fun begins.

A jellyfish waltzes, gracefully mazed,
While plankton chuckle, utterly amazed.
Join the revelry, dive and glide,
In this playful realm, let glee reside!

Sirens of the Deep

Sirens sing with a cheeky charm,
Baiting sailors, causing alarm.
'Come join us here in the deep blue!'
They laugh and wink, it's quite the view.

In seashells, they keep their best jokes,
Making waves with giggling folks.
A splash here, a splash there, oh what fun!
Even the big fish can't help but run.

Flotsam floats with a faint 'hello',
As these sirens plot their wild show.
With bubbles and giggles, they swirl around,
An underwater circus, pure joy abound.

They wave with a wink, hair flowing wide,
In their salty realm, all mischief resides.
So if you hear a sing-song tease,
Remember, it's all just part of the breeze!

Reflection in a Salted Mirror

The tide rolls in with secrets to share,
Reflected laughter bounces in air.
Everyone sees their silly face,
In rippling waters, a comical grace.

Fish poke fun at the clumsy jump,
While sea turtles giggle with a thump.
'Look at that surfer, oh what a sight!'
They chuckle and ponder, is he alright?

A clam concussed with a glimmer of pride,
Opens wide with a snicker inside.
As foam tickles toes, the madness is clear,
In this mirrored jest, everyone's cheer.

So dance with the waves, join the parade,
In the salted mirror, laughter's made.
Each splash of a wave, a jest to perceive,
In this wacky world, we all believe!

Marinara Melancholy

A fish once dreamed of a marinara,
He swam in sauce with a joyful aura.
But when the chef came, oh what a mess!
He yelled, "I'm seafood, not your dress!"

The crabs all danced with pasta in hand,
Giggling at shells in a conga line band.
They twirled and twirled, full of delight,
Until they got caught in a noodle fight!

A dolphin laughed at a seagull's dive,
"You missed your catch! Are you alive?"
The seagull swooped down, with a clever quip,
"I'm just saving energy for my next trip!"

In this watery world, where humor flows,
Even the plankton wear fancy clothes.
So raise your glasses, let's toast and cheer,
To all the jokes that swim far and near!

Rippled Reflections

The waves giggle as they kiss the shore,
Telling secrets, forever wanting more.
A crab with shades sips his coconut drink,
While fish on a trampoline take a leap and blink!

Shells gossip about those lost at sea,
"Did you hear about the fish?" "No, tell it to me!"
While barnacles chuckle, stuck on their rocks,
"Life's a little slow, but we love our talks!"

A surfer dude with jellyfish hair,
Lost his balance, but had not a care.
He slipped and fell with a splash so grand,
Unless he was trying to start a band!

Each ripple carries a story so light,
In this salty realm, there's joy and delight.
So let's dance like seaweed in a swell,
Where laughter and fun cast a magical spell!

Harboring Dreams

A sleepy seal took a nap on a dock,
Dreamt of surfboards and a big ticking clock.
He woke with a start at a loud, loud honk,
"Oh no! That's not my fancy new trunk!"

Ducks in the harbor practicing their quack,
Had a talent show, no one held back.
The winner was a goose, with a hat made of reeds,
Clapped for by fishes, fulfilling their needs.

A fish tried to juggle some shiny sea parts,
But dropped them all, much to the crowd's hearts.
"Stick to swimming!" they all gave a cheer,
And he swam away, still giggling, I fear!

So in this harbor where dreams drift about,
Laughter erupts with each twist and clout.
It's a whimsical place where silliness reigns,
And even the barnacles forget their chains!

Lullabies of the Lagoon

The chirpy frogs croak their soft little tune,
While fireflies wink under the light of the moon.
An octopus with socks jived around,
Making waves while pulling pranks by the pound!

A sleepy turtle hummed in a shell so tight,
"Why'd the crab cross the reef? To own the night!"
Her friends all chuckled, then drifted away,
As stars wiggled down for a brief ocean play.

An otter swam by with bubbles in tow,
"I'm storing my snacks, come join the show!"
His buddies jumped in, what a splashy scene,
Turning the lagoon into a playful machine!

As night winds down and giggles take flight,
The lagoon whispers, 'This is pure delight!'
So rest your eyes under shimmering beams,
And let the water carry your dreams.

Sandcastles of Wonder

In a kingdom made of sand,
I built a tower, oh so grand.
My dragon made of shells sat proud,
Until a wave came, laughing loud.

Seagulls squawked, a curious crowd,
They took my flag, I should have bowed.
With buckets bright and shovels near,
I crafted dreams but lost my cheer.

A crab declared, "You're doing well!"
But he just meant to steal my shell.
I chased it down, kicking up sand,
Only to trip—what a clumsy hand!

But in the end, with laughter's glow,
We danced by seashells in a row.
The tide came in, my castle drowned,
Yet the joy I found will always sound.

Tranquil Tides

The waves are waltzing, a funny sight,
They frolic and bounce with sheer delight.
I tried to surf, a bold idea,
But ended up swimming with a sea deer.

A fish swam by with a cheeky grin,
"Are you here to laugh or to dive in?"
I splashed and sputtered, making a scene,
The seaweed wrapped me like a green bean.

My friends were sunbathing, having a blast,
While I was the one the sea had amassed.
But laughter bubbled like the surf's sweet kiss,
In this watery chaos, I found my bliss.

So if you tire of the normal tide,
Join the fish and let laughter be your guide.
With water balloons and giggles galore,
Life's a silly dance on this sandy shore.

The Glistening Abyss

Beneath the waves, a treasure's glow,
But watch your step, don't go too low!
For lurking down in murky depths,
Are fish that joke while holding their breaths.

A turtle swam with a pirate hat,
Claiming to be a seafoam brat.
He tossed out pearls like they were stones,
While jellyfish jived on their own bones.

I followed a crab in a wild race,
Waving my hands in a frenzied embrace.
But oh dear, he quickened his pace,
Leaving behind a trail of my grace.

Still, in this abyss of salt and fun,
Every splash feels like a silly pun.
So here's to the laughs that the sea bestows,
In every wave, more giggles arose.

Celestial Sailors

The starfish struck a sailor's pose,
While dolphins put on quite the show.
Under the moon's soft, silver glow,
We danced on waves, just letting go.

A lobster wore a tux that shone,
Claiming he wouldn't be outgrown.
He twirled and spun, quite a delight,
Making me laugh through the chilly night.

We raised our glasses filled with seawater,
Toasting to the waves, oh how they falter.
The constellations cheered from above,
As if the stars were in on our love.

So here's to the mariners of the sea,
Who sail along with wild jubilee.
With every wave as a friend to cheer,
Let laughter echo, year after year.

Beneath the Azure Veil

Bubbles rise like laughter here,
Fish wear hats, they disappear.
Crabs can dance, but they won't try,
They pinch my toes; I squeal and cry.

Waves tickle toes, what a tease,
Seagulls swoop down with cheeky ease.
Shells wear smiles, all so bright,
They glitter and giggle in the light.

Mermaids play cards, what a sight,
Their scales shimmer in the night.
Turtles roll with glee and cheer,
As jellyfish twirl without any fear.

A starfish claims the bottom seat,
Says, "No chairs, but oh, what a feat!"
With a wink and a flip of a fin,
They bid me welcome; let fun begin!

Sirens' Serenade

Singing fish with voices high,
They serenade the passing sky.
Octopuses play harp and flute,
While squids give lengthy lessons astute.

A pufferfish puffs up with pride,
Says, "Join the band, come for a ride!"
With scales that shimmer, they sway and spin,
The underwater dance-off is about to begin.

Crabs do the cha-cha while turtles glide,
Snails are slow, but they're full of stride.
With every note, the seafloor shakes,
Even the rocks giggle and break.

As the moonlight shines down so bright,
Mermaids weave dreams with all their might.
They toss glitter to the surface blue,
Join our party, there's room for you!

Currents of Dreaming

Drifting dreams on gentle waves,
Seaweed sways, oh how it braves!
Dolphins giggle as they pass by,
One steals my hat - oh my oh my!

A starfish claims my hammock now,
Says, "You can't sit here, but I'll allow!"
With sea cucumbers doing the twist,
The coral reefs become a bliss.

Sandy shores with castles tall,
A crab is king, he rules us all.
He wears a crown made of shells and sand,
While waves come clapping like a band.

As I drift in this dreamy place,
A clownfish paints a silly face.
With every splash, laughter spills,
In this watery land, joy fulfills!

Echoes in the Deep

Down below the waves so deep,
Giggling fish do not make a peep.
Echoes of laughter fill the sea,
As clowns in shells play tricks on me.

Anemones wave their fuzzy arms,
While seahorses flaunt their charms.
They spin and twirl, a vibrant show,
With bubbles bursting as they go.

A whale thinks he's a pop star here,
Sings off-key, but we all cheer!
Clapping clams keep time with grace,
While grouchy eels make silly face.

With every splash, we burst with glee,
In the depths where fun is free.
The ocean hums a playful tune,
Every creature joins the croon!

Caresses of the Brine

A seal with sunglasses floated by,
He winked with a flipper, oh my!
Fish in tuxedos danced in a line,
As the jellyfish twirled with a smile so fine.

Crabs in a conga, a sight to behold,
Pinching and prancing, so bold!
Lobsters in shades voting for king,
While seagulls debated on the next big fling.

Nautical Journeys

A sailor with socks, a fashion faux pas,
Rode waves like a pro, while eating a straw!
His parrot squawked jokes, what a funny tune,
Sailing past shrimp in a jubilant swoon.

Octopuses served snacks with eight hands,
As dolphins played cards with all their plans!
A treasure map drawn with crayons bright,
Led to a chest filled with bubblegum delight.

Waves Whisper Secrets

The waves giggled softly, sharing sweet tales,
Of pirates lost in their pants and their sails.
Seaweed waved flags, in a cheeky parade,
While starfish cheered from the rocks they'd invade.

Mermaids played tag with the boys of the tide,
But ended up losing their shells and their pride!
The tidepool's laughter, a bubbly delight,
As crabs contemplated their next dance tonight.

Tides of Transcendence

When the tide rolled in, with a splash and a giggle,
Anemones jived to the seaweed's big wiggle.
Clams cracked up at the fish in a chase,
While dolphins suggested an ocean-wide race.

A whale wore a hat made of sea foam and glee,
As barnacles clapped by the coral's decree.
The laughter of scallops echoed around,
In a watery world where joy knows no bound.

Currents of Reverie

Fish wear glasses, fish wear hats,
Riding seahorses, where's my cat?
Octopus juggling, quite the show,
Seagulls squawking, stealing my dough!

Waves that giggle, splash with glee,
Chasing bubbles, just like me.
Starfish dance, with fins so bright,
Mermaids laughing, what a sight!

Aquatic Fantasia

Crabs in tuxedos, ready to dine,
Shrimp on the menu, oh how divine!
Jellyfish bouncing, like they're on air,
Dolphins whisper, secrets to share.

Seashells chatting, gossip so sweet,
Anemones weaving, tapestries neat.
Clownfish chuckling, making a scene,
Life underwater, like a daydream!

Tempest and Tranquility

Whirlwinds swirling, hats go flying,
Mermaids diving, people sighing.
A lighthouse blinks, like a disco ball,
Seals playing tag, we all have a ball!

Raindrops tap dance, a rhythm of fun,
Storm clouds frown, still we all run.
Umbrellas sail, like pirate's quest,
Waves of laughter, we feel so blessed!

Watercolors of the Deep

Crayons at seaside, colors galore,
Rainbow fishes dash, who could ask for more?
An artist shark splashes blue all around,
While drum-playing turtles keep groovy sound.

Coral reefs flipping, like pages in a book,
Each fish a story, come take a look!
Aquatic waltz, a whimsical flight,
Beneath the waves, everything feels right!

www.ingramcontent.com/pod-product-compliance
Lightning Source LLC
Chambersburg PA
CBHW060146230426
43661CB00003B/597